The War Poems by Siegfried Sassoon

Siegfried Loraine Sassoon was born on 8th September 1886.

Sassoon was educated at the New Beacon School, Sevenoaks, Kent then Marlborough College, Wiltshire and finally at Clare College, Cambridge, where from 1905 to 1907 he read history. He went down from Cambridge without a degree and spent the next few years indulging himself hunting, playing cricket and writing verse.

However, motivated by patriotism, Sassoon joined the Sussex Yeomanry of the British Army as the threat of war escalated into open conflict.

His early poems exhibit a Romantic, dilettantish sweetness but his war poetry moves to an increasingly discordant beat, stridently conveying the ugly truths of the trenches to an audience hitherto placated by jingoistic and patriotic propaganda.

Sassoon's periods of duty on the Western Front were marked by near-suicidal missions, including the single-handed capture of a German trench. Armed with grenades, he scattered sixty German soldiers.

In 1919 took up a post as literary editor of the socialist Daily Herald. Here he was responsible for employing several eminent reviewers, including E. M. Forster and Charlotte Mew. Sassoon also commissioned new material from the likes of Arnold Bennett and Osbert Sitwell.

Sassoon was now, in 1928, preparing to take a new direction by branching out into prose, with 'Memoirs of a Fox-Hunting Man'. This anonymously published first volume of a fictionalised autobiography, was acclaimed as a classic, bringing its author fame as a humorous writer. Other volumes including his own autobiography based on his youth and early manhood across three volumes followed.

In his last years Sassoon converted to Roman Catholicism and was admitted to the faith at Downside Abbey in Somerset.

Siegfried Loraine Sassoon, CBE, MC died from stomach cancer on 1st September 1967, a week before his 81st birthday.

Index of Contents

PART I

PRELUDE: THE TROOPS

Dim, gradual thinning of the shapeless gloom
Shudders to drizzling daybreak that reveals
Disconsolate men who stamp their sodden boots
And turn dulled, sunken faces to the sky
Haggard and hopeless. They, who have beaten down
The stale despair of night, must now renew
Their desolation in the truce of dawn,
Murdering the livid hours that grope for peace.

Yet these, who cling to life with stubborn hands,
Can grin through storms of death and find a gap
In the clawed, cruel tangles of his defence.
They march from safety, and the bird-sung joy
Of grass-green thickets, to the land where all
Is ruin, and nothing blossoms but the sky
That hastens over them where they endure
Sad, smoking, flat horizons, reeking woods,
And foundered trench-lines volleying doom for doom.

O my brave brown companions, when your souls
Flock silently away, and the eyeless dead,
Shame the wild beast of battle on the ridge,
Death will stand grieving in that field of war
Since your unvanquished hardihood is spent.
And through some mooned Valhalla there will pass
Battalions and battalions, scarred from hell;
The unreturning army that was youth;
The legions who have suffered and are dust.

DREAMERS

Soldiers are citizens of death's gray land,
Drawing no dividend from time's to-morrows.
In the great hour of destiny they stand,
Each with his feuds, and jealousies, and sorrows.
Soldiers are sworn to action; they must win
Some flaming, fatal climax with their lives.
Soldiers are dreamers; when the guns begin
They think of firelit homes, clean beds, and wives.

I see them in foul dug-outs, gnawed by rats,
And in the ruined trenches, lashed with rain,
Dreaming of things they did with balls and bats,
And mocked by hopeless longing to regain
Bank-holidays, and picture shows, and spats,
And going to the office in the train.

THE REDEEMER

Darkness: the rain sluiced down; the mire was deep;
It was past twelve on a mid-winter night,
When peaceful folk in beds lay snug asleep:
There, with much work to do before the light,
We lugged our clay-sucked boots as best we might
Along the trench; sometimes a bullet sang,
And droning shells burst with a hollow bang;
We were soaked, chilled and wretched, every one.
Darkness: the distant wink of a huge gun.

I turned in the black ditch, loathing the storm;
A rocket fizzed and burned with blanching flare,
And lit the face of what had been a form
Floundering in mirk. He stood before me there;
I say that he was Christ; stiff in the glare,
And leaning forward from his burdening task,
Both arms supporting it; his eyes on mine
Stared from the woeful head that seemed a mask
Of mortal pain in Hell's unholy shine.

No thorny crown, only a woollen cap
He wore—an English soldier, white and strong,
Who loved his time like any simple chap,
Good days of work and sport and homely song;
Now he has learned that nights are very long,

And dawn a watching of the windowed sky.
But to the end, unjudging, he'll endure
Horror and pain, not uncontent to die
That Lancaster on Lune may stand secure.

He faced me, reeling in his weariness,
Shouldering his load of planks, so hard to bear.
I say that he was Christ, who wrought to bless
All groping things with freedom bright as air,
And with His mercy washed and made them fair.
Then the flame sank, and all grew black as pitch,
While we began to struggle along the ditch;
And some one flung his burden in the muck,
Mumbling: "O Christ Almighty, now I'm stuck!"

TRENCH DUTY

Shaken from sleep, and numbed and scarce awake,
Out in the trench with three hours' watch to take,
I blunder through the splashing mirk; and then
Hear the gruff muttering voices of the men
Crouching in cabins candle-chinked with light.
Hark! There's the big bombardment on our right
Rumbling and bumping; and the dark's a glare
Of flickering horror in the sectors where
We raid the Boche; men waiting, stiff and chilled,
Or crawling on their bellies through the wire.
"What? Stretcher-bearers wanted? Some one killed?"
Five minutes ago I heard a sniper fire:
Why did he do it?... Starlight overhead—
Blank stars. I'm wide-awake; and some chap's dead.

WIRERS

"Pass it along, the wiring party's going out"—
And yawning sentries mumble, "Wirers going out."
Unravelling; twisting; hammering stakes with muffled thud,
They toil with stealthy haste and anger in their blood.

The Boche sends up a flare. Black forms stand rigid there,
Stock-still like posts; then darkness, and the clumsy ghosts
Stride hither and thither, whispering, tripped by clutching snare
Of snags and tangles.
Ghastly dawn with vaporous coasts

Gleams desolate along the sky, night's misery ended.

Young Hughes was badly hit; I heard him carried away,
Moaning at every lurch; no doubt he'll die to-day.
But we can say the front-line wire's been safely mended.

BREAK OF DAY

There seemed a smell of autumn in the air
At the bleak end of night; he shivered there
In a dank, musty dug-out where he lay,
Legs wrapped in sand-bags,—lumps of chalk and clay
Spattering his face. Dry-mouthed, he thought, "To-day
We start the damned attack; and, Lord knows why,
Zero's at nine; how bloody if I'm done in
Under the freedom of that morning sky!"
And then he coughed and dozed, cursing the din.

Was it the ghost of autumn in that smell
Of underground, or God's blank heart grown kind,
That sent a happy dream to him in hell?—
Where men are crushed like clods, and crawl to find
Some crater for their wretchedness; who lie
In outcast immolation, doomed to die
Far from clean things or any hope of cheer,
Cowed anger in their eyes, till darkness brims
And roars into their heads, and they can hear
Old childish talk, and tags of foolish hymns.

He sniffs the chilly air; (his dreaming starts).
He's riding in a dusty Sussex lane
In quiet September; slowly night departs;
And he's a living soul, absolved from pain.
Beyond the brambled fences where he goes
Are glimmering fields with harvest piled in sheaves,
And tree-tops dark against the stars grown pale;
Then, clear and shrill, a distant farm-cock crows;
And there's a wall of mist along the vale
Where willows shake their watery-sounding leaves.
He gazes on it all, and scarce believes
That earth is telling its old peaceful tale;
He thanks the blessed world that he was born....
Then, far away, a lonely note of the horn.

They're drawing the Big Wood! Unlatch the gate,
And set Golumpus going on the grass:

He knows the corner where it's best to wait
And hear the crashing woodland chorus pass;
The corner where old foxes make their track
To the Long Spinney; that's the place to be.
The bracken shakes below an ivied tree,
And then a cub looks out; and "Tally-o-back!"
He bawls, and swings his thong with volleying crack,—
All the clean thrill of autumn in his blood,
And hunting surging through him like a flood
In joyous welcome from the untroubled past;
While the war drifts away, forgotten at last.

Now a red, sleepy sun above the rim
Of twilight stares along the quiet weald,
And the kind, simple country shines revealed
In solitudes of peace, no longer dim.
The old horse lifts his face and thanks the light,
Then stretches down his head to crop the green.
All things that he has loved are in his sight;
The places where his happiness has been
Are in his eyes, his heart, and they are good.

Hark! there's the horn: they're drawing the Big Wood.

A WORKING PARTY

Three hours ago he blundered up the trench,
Sliding and poising, groping with his boots;
Sometimes he tripped and lurched against the walls
With hands that pawed the sodden bags of chalk.
He couldn't see the man who walked in front;
Only he heard the drum and rattle of feet
Stepping along the trench-boards,—often splashing
Wretchedly where the sludge was ankle-deep.

Voices would grunt, "Keep to your right,—make way!"
When squeezing past the men from the front-line:
White faces peered, puffing a point of red;
Candles and braziers glinted through the chinks
And curtain-flaps of dug-outs; then the gloom
Swallowed his sense of sight; he stooped and swore
Because a sagging wire had caught his neck.
A flare went up; the shining whiteness spread
And flickered upward, showing nimble rats,
And mounds of glimmering sand-bags, bleached with rain;
Then the slow, silver moment died in dark.

The wind came posting by with chilly gusts
And buffeting at corners, piping thin
And dreary through the crannies; rifle-shots
Would split and crack and sing along the night,
And shells came calmly through the drizzling air
To burst with hollow bang below the hill.

Three hours ago he stumbled up the trench;
Now he will never walk that road again:
He must be carried back, a jolting lump
Beyond all need of tenderness and care;
A nine-stone corpse with nothing more to do.

He was a young man with a meagre wife
And two pale children in a Midland town;
He showed the photograph to all his mates;
And they considered him a decent chap
Who did his work and hadn't much to say,
And always laughed at other people's jokes
Because he hadn't any of his own.

That night, when he was busy at his job
Of piling bags along the parapet,
He thought how slow time went, stamping his feet,
And blowing on his fingers, pinched with cold.

He thought of getting back by half-past twelve,
And tot of rum to send him warm to sleep
In draughty dug-out frowsty with the fumes
Of coke, and full of snoring, weary men.

He pushed another bag along the top,
Craning his body outward; then a flare
Gave one white glimpse of No Man's Land and wire;
And as he dropped his head the instant split
His startled life with lead, and all went out.

STAND-TO: GOOD FRIDAY MORNING

I'd been on duty from two till four.
I went and stared at the dug-out door.
Down in the frowst I heard them snore.
"Stand-to!" Somebody grunted and swore.
Dawn was misty; the skies were still;
Larks were singing, discordant, shrill;

They seemed happy; but I felt ill.
Deep in water I splashed my way
Up the trench to our bogged front line.
Rain had fallen the whole damned night.
O Jesus, send me a wound to-day,
And I'll believe in Your bread and wine,
And get my bloody old sins washed white!

"IN THE PINK"

So Davies wrote: "This leaves me in the pink."
Then scrawled his name: "Your loving sweetheart, Willie."
With crosses for a hug. He'd had a drink
Of rum and tea; and, though the barn was chilly,
For once his blood ran warm; he had pay to spend.
Winter was passing; soon the year would mend.

He couldn't sleep that night. Stiff in the dark
He groaned and thought of Sundays at the farm,
When he'd go out as cheerful as a lark
In his best suit to wander arm-in-arm
With brown-eyed Gwen, and whisper in her ear
The simple, silly things she liked to hear.

And then he thought: to-morrow night we trudge
Up to the trenches, and my boots are rotten.
Five miles of stodgy clay and freezing sludge,
And everything but wretchedness forgotten.
To-night he's in the pink; but soon he'll die.
And still the war goes on; he don't know why.

THE HERO

"Jack fell as he'd have wished," the Mother said,
And folded up the letter that she'd read.
"The Colonel writes so nicely." Something broke
In the tired voice that quavered to a choke.
She half looked up. "We mothers are so proud
Of our dead soldiers." Then her face was bowed.

Quietly the Brother Officer went out.
He'd told the poor old dear some gallant lies
That she would nourish all her days, no doubt.
For while he coughed and mumbled, her weak eyes

Had shone with gentle triumph, brimmed with joy,
Because he'd been so brave, her glorious boy.

He thought how "Jack," cold-footed, useless swine,
Had panicked down the trench that night the mine
Went up at Wicked Corner; how he'd tried
To get sent home; and how, at last, he died,
Blown to small bits. And no one seemed to care
Except that lonely woman with white hair.

BEFORE THE BATTLE

Music of whispering trees
Hushed by the broad-winged breeze
Where shaken water gleams;
And evening radiance falling
With reedy bird-notes calling.
O bear me safe through dark, you low-voiced streams.

I have no need to pray
That fear may pass away;
I scorn the growl and rumble of the fight
That summons me from cool
Silence of marsh and pool,
And yellow lilies islanded in light.
O river of stars and shadows, lead me through the night.

June 25th, 1916.

THE ROAD

The road is thronged with women; soldiers pass
And halt, but never see them; yet they're here—
A patient crowd along the sodden grass,
Silent, worn out with waiting, sick with fear.
The road goes crawling up a long hillside,
All ruts and stones and sludge, and the emptied dregs
Of battle thrown in heaps. Here where they died
Are stretched big-bellied horses with stiff legs;
And dead men, bloody-fingered from the fight,
Stare up at caverned darkness winking white.

You in the bomb-scorched kilt, poor sprawling Jock,
You tottered here and fell, and stumbled on,

Half dazed for want of sleep. No dream could mock
Your reeling brain with comforts lost and gone.
You did not feel her arms about your knees,
Her blind caress, her lips upon your head:
Too tired for thoughts of home and love and ease,
The road would serve you well enough for bed.

TWO HUNDRED YEARS AFTER

Trudging by Corbie Ridge one winter's night,
(Unless old, hearsay memories tricked his sight),
Along the pallid edge of the quiet sky
He watched a nosing lorry grinding on,
And straggling files of men; when these were gone,
A double limber and six mules went by,
Hauling the rations up through ruts and mud
To trench-lines digged two hundred years ago.
Then darkness hid them with a rainy scud,
And soon he saw the village lights below.

But when he'd told his tale, an old man said
That he'd seen soldiers pass along that hill;
"Poor, silent things, they were the English dead
Who came to fight in France and got their fill."

THE DREAM

I

Moonlight and dew-drenched blossom, and the scent
Of summer gardens; these can bring you all
Those dreams that in the starlit silence fall:
Sweet songs are full of odours.
While I went
Last night in drizzling dusk along a lane,
I passed a squalid farm; from byre and midden
Came the rank smell that brought me once again
A dream of war that in the past was hidden.

II

Up a disconsolate straggling village street
I saw the tired troops trudge: I heard their feet.

The cheery Q.M.S. was there to meet
And guide our Company in....
I watched them stumble.
Into some crazy hovel, too beat to grumble;
Saw them file inward, slipping from their backs
Rifles, equipment, packs.

On filthy straw they sit in the gloom, each face
Bowed to patched, sodden boots they must unlace,
While the wind chills their sweat through chinks and cracks.

III

I'm looking at their blistered feet; young Jones
Stares up at me, mud-splashed and white and jaded;
Out of his eyes the morning light has faded.
Old soldiers with three winters in their bones
Puff their damp Woodbines, whistle, stretch their toes
They can still grin at me, for each of 'em knows
That I'm as tired as they are....
Can they guess
The secret burden that is always mine?—
Pride in their courage; pity for their distress;
And burning bitterness
That I must take them to the accursèd Line.

IV

I cannot hear their voices, but I see
Dim candles in the barn: they gulp their tea,
And soon they'll sleep like logs. Ten miles away
The battle winks and thuds in blundering strife.
And I must lead them nearer, day by day,
To the foul beast of war that bludgeons life.

AT CARNOY

Down in the hollow there's the whole Brigade
Camped in four groups: through twilight falling slow
I hear a sound of mouth-organs, ill-played,
And murmur of voices, gruff, confused, and low.
Crouched among thistle-tufts I've watched the glow
Of a blurred orange sunset flare and fade;
And I'm content. To-morrow we must go

To take some cursèd Wood.... O world God made!

July 3rd, 1916.

BATTALION RELIEF

"Fall in! Now, get a move on!" (Curse the rain.)
We splash away along the straggling village,
Out to the flat rich country green with June....
And sunset flares across wet crops and tillage,
Blazing with splendour-patches. Harvest soon
Up in the Line. "Perhaps the War'll be done
By Christmas-time. Keep smiling then, old son!"

Here's the Canal: it's dusk; we cross the bridge.
"Lead on there by platoons." The Line's a-glare
With shell-fire through the poplars; distant rattle
Of rifles and machine-guns. "Fritz is there!
Christ, ain't it lively, Sergeant? Is't a battle?"
More rain: the lightning blinks, and thunder rumbles.
"There's overhead artillery," some chap grumbles.

"What's all this mob, by the cross-road?" (The guides)....
"Lead on with Number One" (And off they go.)

"Three-minute intervals." ... Poor blundering files,
Sweating and blindly burdened; who's to know
If death will catch them in those two dark miles?
(More rain.) "Lead on, Headquarters."
(That's the lot.)
"Who's that? O, Sergeant-major; don't get shot!
And tell me, have we won this war or not?"

THE DUG-OUT

Why do you lie with your legs ungainly huddled,
And one arm bent across your sullen cold
Exhausted face? It hurts my heart to watch you,
Deep-shadow'd from the candle's guttering gold;
And you wonder why I shake you by the shoulder;
Drowsy, you mumble and sigh and turn your head....
You are too young to fall asleep for ever;
And when you sleep you remind me of the dead.

THE REAR-GUARD

(Hindenburg Line, April 1917)

Groping along the tunnel, step by step,
He winked his prying torch with patching glare
From side to side, and sniffed the unwholesome air.

Tins, boxes, bottles, shapes too vague to know,
A mirror smashed, the mattress from a bed;
And he, exploring fifty feet below
The rosy gloom of battle overhead.

Tripping, he grabbed the wall; saw some one lie
Humped at his feet, half-hidden by a rug,
And stooped to give the sleeper's arm a tug.
"I'm looking for headquarters." No reply.
"God blast your neck!" (For days he'd had no sleep,)
"Get up and guide me through this stinking place."
Savage, he kicked a soft, unanswering heap,
And flashed his beam across the livid face
Terribly glaring up, whose eyes yet wore
Agony dying hard ten days before;
And fists of fingers clutched a blackening wound.

Alone he staggered on until he found
Dawn's ghost that filtered down a shafted stair
To the dazed, muttering creatures underground
Who hear the boom of shells in muffled sound.
At last, with sweat of horror in his hair,
He climbed through darkness to the twilight air,
Unloading hell behind him step by step.

I STOOD WITH THE DEAD

I stood with the Dead, so forsaken and still:
When dawn was grey I stood with the Dead.
And my slow heart said, "You must kill; you must kill:
Soldier, soldier, morning is red."

On the shapes of the slain in their crumpled disgrace
I stared for a while through the thin cold rain....
"O lad that I loved, there is rain on your face,
And your eyes are blurred and sick like the plain."

I stood with the Dead.... They were dead; they were dead;
My heart and my head beat a march of dismay;
And gusts of the wind came dulled by the guns....
"Fall in!" I shouted; "Fall in for your pay!"

SUICIDE IN TRENCHES

I knew a simple soldier boy
Who grinned at life in empty joy,
Slept soundly through the lonesome dark,
And whistled early with the lark.

In winter trenches, cowed and glum
With crumps and lice and lack of rum,
He put a bullet through his brain.
No one spoke of him again.

You smug-faced crowds with kindling eye
Who cheer when soldier lads march by,
Sneak home and pray you'll never know
The hell where youth and laughter go.

ATTACK

At dawn the ridge emerges massed and dun
In the wild purple of the glowering sun
Smouldering through spouts of drifting smoke that shroud
The menacing scarred slope; and, one by one,
Tanks creep and topple forward to the wire.
The barrage roars and lifts. Then, clumsily bowed
With bombs and guns and shovels and battle-gear,
Men jostle and climb to meet the bristling fire.
Lines of grey, muttering faces, masked with fear,
They leave their trenches, going over the top,
While time ticks blank and busy on their wrists,
And hope, with furtive eyes and grappling fists,
Flounders in mud. O Jesu, make it stop!

COUNTER-ATTACK

We'd gained our first objective hours before

While dawn broke like a face with blinking eyes,
Pallid, unshaved and thirsty, blind with smoke.
Things seemed all right at first. We held their line,
With bombers posted, Lewis guns well placed,
And clink of shovels deepening the shallow trench.
The place was rotten with dead; green clumsy legs
High-booted, sprawled and grovelled along the saps
And trunks, face downward in the sucking mud,
Wallowed like trodden sand-bags loosely filled;
And naked sodden buttocks, mats of hair,
Bulged, clotted heads, slept in the plastering slime.
And then the rain began,—the jolly old rain!

A yawning soldier knelt against the bank,
Staring across the morning blear with fog;
He wondered when the Allemands would get busy;
And then, of course, they started with five-nines
Traversing, sure as fate, and never a dud.
Mute in the clamour of shells he watched them burst
Spouting dark earth and wire with gusts from hell,
While posturing giants dissolved in drifts of smoke.

He crouched and flinched, dizzy with galloping fear,
Sick for escape,—loathing the strangled horror
And butchered, frantic gestures of the dead.

An officer came blundering down the trench:
"Stand-to and man the fire-step!" On he went....
Gasping and bawling, "Fire-step ... counter-attack!"
Then the haze lifted. Bombing on the right
Down the old sap: machine-guns on the left;
And stumbling figures looming out in front.
"O Christ, they're coming at us!" Bullets spat,
And he remembered his rifle ... rapid fire ...
And started blazing wildly ... then a bang
Crumpled and spun him sideways, knocked him out
To grunt and wriggle: none heeded him; he choked
And fought the flapping veils of smothering gloom,
Lost in a blurred confusion of yells and groans....
Down, and down, and down, he sank and drowned,
Bleeding to death. The counter-attack had failed.

THE EFFECT

"The effect of our bombardment was terrific. One man told me he had never seen so many dead before."
War Correspondent.

"He'd never seen so many dead before."
They sprawled in yellow daylight while he swore
And gasped and lugged his everlasting load
Of bombs along what once had been a road.
"How peaceful are the dead."
Who put that silly gag in some one's head?

"He'd never seen so many dead before."
The lilting words danced up and down his brain,
While corpses jumped and capered in the rain.
No, no; he wouldn't count them any more....
The dead have done with pain:
They've choked; they can't come back to life again.

When Dick was killed last week he looked like that,
Flapping along the fire-step like a fish,
After the blazing crump had knocked him flat....
"How many dead? As many as ever you wish.
Don't count 'em; they're too many.
Who'll buy my nice fresh corpses, two a penny?"

REMORSE

Lost in the swamp and welter of the pit,
He flounders off the duck-boards; only he knows
Each flash and spouting crash,—each instant lit
When gloom reveals the streaming rain. He goes
Heavily, blindly on. And, while he blunders,
"Could anything be worse than this?"—he wonders,
Remembering how he saw those Germans run,
Screaming for mercy among the stumps of trees:
Green-faced, they dodged and darted: there was one
Livid with terror, clutching at his knees....
Our chaps were sticking 'em like pigs.... "O hell!"
He thought—"there's things in war one dare not tell
Poor father sitting safe at home, who reads
Of dying heroes and their deathless deeds."

IN AN UNDERGROUND DRESSING-STATION

Quietly they set their burden down: he tried
To grin; moaned; moved his head from side to side.

He gripped the stretcher; stiffened; glared; and screamed,
"O put my leg down, doctor, do!" (He'd got
A bullet in his ankle; and he'd been shot
Horribly through the guts.) The surgeon seemed
So kind and gentle, saying, above that crying,
"You must keep still, my lad." But he was dying.

DIED OF WOUNDS

His wet, white face and miserable eyes
Brought nurses to him more than groans and sighs:
But hoarse and low and rapid rose and fell
His troubled voice: he did the business well.

The ward grew dark; but he was still complaining,
And calling out for "Dickie." "Curse the Wood!
It's time to go; O Christ, and what's the good?—
We'll never take it; and it's always raining."

I wondered where he'd been; then heard him shout,
"They snipe like hell! O Dickie, don't go out" ...
I fell asleep ... next morning he was dead;
And some Slight Wound lay smiling on his bed.

PART II

"THEY"

The Bishop tells us: "When the boys come back
They will not be the same; for they'll have fought
In a just cause: they lead the last attack
On Anti-Christ; their comrade's blood has bought
New right to breed an honourable race.
They have challenged Death and dared him face to face."

"We're none of us the same!" the boys reply.
"For George lost both his legs; and Bill's stone blind;
Poor Jim's shot through the lungs and like to die;
And Bert's gone syphilitic: you'll not find
A chap who's served that hasn't found some change."
And the Bishop said; "The ways of God are strange!"

BASE DETAILS

If I were fierce, and bald, and short of breath,
I'd live with scarlet Majors at the Base,
And speed glum heroes up the line to death.
You'd see me with my puffy petulant face,
Guzzling and gulping in the best hotel,
Reading the Roll of Honour. "Poor young chap,"
I'd say—"I used to know his father well;
Yes, we've lost heavily in this last scrap."
And when the war is done and youth stone dead,
I'd toddle safely home and die—in bed.

LAMENTATIONS

I found him in a guard-room at the Base.
From the blind darkness I had heard his crying
And blundered in. With puzzled, patient face
A sergeant watched him; it was no good trying
To stop it; for he howled and beat his chest.
And, all because his brother had gone West,
Raved at the bleeding war; his rampant grief
Moaned, shouted, sobbed, and choked, while he was kneeling
Half-naked on the floor. In my belief
Such men have lost all patriotic feeling.

THE GENERAL

"Good-morning; good-morning!" the General said
When we met him last week on our way to the Line,
Now the soldiers he smiled at are most of 'em dead,
And we're cursing his staff for incompetent swine.
"He's a cheery old card," grunted Harry to Jack
As they slogged up to Arras with rifle and pack.

But he did for them both by his plan of attack.

HOW TO DIE

Dark clouds are smouldering into red
While down the craters morning burns.

The dying soldier shifts his head
To watch the glory that returns:
He lifts his fingers toward the skies
Where holy brightness breaks in flame;
Radiance reflected in his eyes,
And on his lips a whispered name.

You'd think, to hear some people talk,
That lads go West with sobs and curses,
And sullen faces white as chalk,
Hankering for wreaths and tombs and hearses.
But they've been taught the way to do it
Like Christian soldiers; not with haste
And shuddering groans; but passing through it
With due regard for decent taste.

EDITORIAL IMPRESSION

He seemed so certain "all was going well,"
As he discussed the glorious time he'd had
While visiting the trenches.
"One can tell
You've gathered big impressions!" grinned the lad
Who'd been severely wounded in the back
In some wiped-out impossible Attack.
"Impressions? Yes, most vivid! I am writing
A little book called Europe on the Rack,
Based on notes made while witnessing the fighting.
I hope I've caught the feeling of 'the Line,'
And the amazing spirit of the troops.
By Jove, those flying-chaps of ours are fine!
I watched one daring beggar looping loops,
Soaring and diving like some bird of prey.
And through it all I felt that splendour shine
Which makes us win."
The soldier sipped his wine.
"Ah, yes, but it's the Press that leads the way!"

FIGHT TO A FINISH

The boys came back. Bands played and flags were flying,
And Yellow-Pressmen thronged the sunlit street
To cheer the soldiers who'd refrained from dying,
And hear the music of returning feet.

"Of all the thrills and ardours War has brought,
This moment is the finest." (So they thought.)

Snapping their bayonets on to charge the mob,
Grim Fusiliers broke ranks with glint of steel.
At last the boys had found a cushy job.

I heard the Yellow-Pressmen grunt and squeal;
And with my trusty bombers turned and went
To clear those Junkers out of Parliament.

ATROCITIES

You told me, in your drunken-boasting mood,
How once you butchered prisoners. That was good!
I'm sure you felt no pity while they stood
Patient and cowed and scared, as prisoners should.

How did you do them in? Come, don't be shy:
You know I love to hear how Germans die,
Downstairs in dug-outs. "Camerad!" they cry;
Then squeal like stoats when bombs begin to fly.

And you? I know your record. You went sick
When orders looked unwholesome: then, with trick
And lie, you wangled home. And here you are,
Still talking big and boozing in a bar.

THE FATHERS

Snug at the club two fathers sat,
Gross, goggle-eyed, and full of chat.
One of them said: "My eldest lad
Writes cheery letters from Bagdad.
But Arthur's getting all the fun
At Arras with his nine-inch gun."

"Yes," wheezed the other, "that's the luck!
My boy's quite broken-hearted, stuck
In England training all this year.
Still, if there's truth in what we hear,
The Huns intend to ask for more
Before they bolt across the Rhine."
I watched them toddle through the door—

These impotent old friends of mine.

"BLIGHTERS"

The house is crammed: tier beyond tier they grin
And cackle at the Show, while prancing ranks
Of harlots shrill the chorus, drunk with din;
"We're sure the Kaiser loves the dear old Tanks!"

I'd like to see a Tank come down the stalls,
Lurching to rag-time tunes, or "Home, sweet Home,"—
And there'd be no more jokes in Music-halls
To mock the riddled corpses round Bapaume.

GLORY OF WOMEN

You love us when we're heroes, home on leave,
Or wounded in a mentionable place.
You worship decorations; you believe
That chivalry redeems the war's disgrace.
You make us shells. You listen with delight,
By tales of dirt and danger fondly thrilled.
You crown our distant ardours while we fight,
And mourn our laurelled memories when we're killed.

You can't believe that British troops "retire"
When hell's last horror breaks them, and they run,
Trampling the terrible corpses—blind with blood.
O German mother dreaming by the fire,
While you are knitting socks to send your son
His face is trodden deeper in the mud.

THEIR FRAILTY

He's got a Blighty wound. He's safe; and then
War's fine and bold and bright.
She can forget the doomed and prisoned men
Who agonize and fight.

He's back in France. She loathes the listless strain
And peril of his plight.
Beseeching Heaven to send him home again,

She prays for peace each night.

Husbands and sons and lovers; everywhere
They die; War bleeds us white.
Mothers and wives and sweethearts,—they don't care
So long as He's all right.

DOES IT MATTER?

Does it matter?—losing your legs?...
For people will always be kind,
And you need not show that you mind
When the others come in after football
To gobble their muffins and eggs.

Does it matter?—losing your sight?...
There's such splendid work for the blind;
And people will always be kind,
As you sit on the terrace remembering
And turning your face to the light.

Do they matter?—those dreams from the pit?...
You can drink and forget and be glad,
And people won't say that you're mad;
For they'll know that you've fought for your country,
And no one will worry a bit.

SURVIVORS

No doubt they'll soon get well; the shock and strain
Have caused their stammering, disconnected talk.
Of course they're "longing to go out again,"—
These boys with old, scared faces, learning to walk,
They'll soon forget their haunted nights; their cowed
Subjection to the ghosts of friends who died,—
Their dreams that drip with murder; and they'll be proud
Of glorious war that shatter'd all their pride....
Men who went out to battle, grim and glad;
Children, with eyes that hate you, broken and mad.

CRAIGLOCKHART,
Oct. 1917.

JOY-BELLS

Ring your sweet bells; but let them be farewells
To the green-vista'd gladness of the past
That changed us into soldiers; swing your bells
To a joyful chime; but let it be the last.

What means this metal in windy belfries hung
When guns are all our need? Dissolve these bells
Whose tones are tuned for peace: with martial tongue
Let them cry doom and storm the sun with shells.

Bells are like fierce-browed prelates who proclaim
That "if our Lord returned He'd fight for us."
So let our bells and bishops do the same,
Shoulder to shoulder with the motor-bus.

ARMS AND THE MAN

Young Croesus went to pay his call
On Colonel Sawbones, Caxton Hall:
And, though his wound was healed and mended,
He hoped he'd get his leave extended.

The waiting-room was dark and bare.
He eyed a neat-framed notice there
Above the fireplace hung to show
Disabled heroes where to go
For arms and legs; with scale of price,
And words of dignified advice
How officers could get them free.

Elbow or shoulder, hip or knee,—
Two arms, two legs, though all were lost,
They'd be restored him free of cost.

Then a Girl-Guide looked in to say,
"Will Captain Croesus come this way?"

WHEN I'M AMONG A BLAZE OF LIGHTS

When I'm among a blaze of lights,
With tawdry music and cigars

And women dawdling through delights,
And officers at cocktail bars,—
Sometimes I think of garden nights
And elm trees nodding at the stars.

I dream of a small firelit room
With yellow candles burning straight,
And glowing pictures in the gloom,
And kindly books that hold me late.
Of things like these I love to think
When I can never be alone:
Then some one says, "Another drink?"—
And turns my living heart to stone.

THE KISS

To these I turn, in these I trust;
Brother Lead and Sister Steel.
To his blind power I make appeal;
I guard her beauty clean from rust.

He spins and burns and loves the air,
And splits a skull to win my praise;
But up the nobly marching days
She glitters naked, cold and fair.

Sweet Sister, grant your soldier this;
That in good fury he may feel
The body where he sets his heel
Quail from your downward darting kiss.

THE TOMBSTONE-MAKER

He primmed his loose red mouth, and leaned his head
Against a sorrowing angel's breast, and said:
"You'd think so much bereavement would have made
Unusual big demands upon my trade.
The War comes cruel hard on some poor folk—
Unless the fighting stops I'll soon be broke."

He eyed the Cemetery across the road—
"There's scores of bodies out abroad, this while,
That should be here by rights; they little know'd
How they'd get buried in such wretched style."

I told him, with a sympathetic grin,
That Germans boil dead soldiers down for fat;
And he was horrified. "What shameful sin!
O sir, that Christian men should come to that!"

THE ONE-LEGGED MAN

Propped on a stick he viewed the August weald;
Squat orchard trees and oasts with painted cowls;
A homely, tangled hedge, a corn-stooked field,
With sound of barking dogs and farmyard fowls.

And he'd come home again to find it more
Desirable than ever it was before.
How right it seemed that he should reach the span
Of comfortable years allowed to man!

Splendid to eat and sleep and choose a wife,
Safe with his wound, a citizen of life.
He hobbled blithely through the garden gate,
And thought; "Thank God they had to amputate!"

RETURN OF THE HEROES

A lady watches from the crowd,
Enthusiastic, flushed, and proud.

"Oh! there's Sir Henry Dudster! Such a splendid leader!
How pleased he looks! What rows of ribbons on his tunic!
Such dignity.... Saluting.... (Wave your flag ... now, Freda!)...
Yes, dear, I saw a Prussian General once,—at Munich.

"Here's the next carriage!... Jack was once in Leggit's Corps;
That's him!... I think the stout one is Sir Godfrey Stoomer.
They must feel sad to know they can't win any more
Great victories!... Aren't they glorious men?... so full of humour!"

PART III

TWELVE MONTHS AFTER

Hullo! here's my platoon, the lot I had last year.
"The War'll be over soon."
"What 'opes?"
"No bloody fear!"
Then, "Number Seven, 'shun! All present and correct."
They're standing in the sun, impassive and erect.
Young Gibson with his grin; and Morgan, tired and white;
Jordan, who's out to win a D.C.M. some night:
And Hughes that's keen on wiring; and Davies ('79),
Who always must be firing at the Boche front line.

"Old soldiers never die; they simply fide a-why!"
That's what they used to sing along the roads last spring;
That's what they used to say before the push began;
That's where they are to-day, knocked over to a man.

TO ANY DEAD OFFICER

Well, how are things in Heaven? I wish you'd say,
Because I'd like to know that you're all right.
Tell me, have you found everlasting day,
Or been sucked in by everlasting night?
For when I shut my eyes your face shows plain;
I hear you make some cheery old remark—
I can rebuild you in my brain,
Though you've gone out patrolling in the dark.

You hated tours of trenches; you were proud
Of nothing more than having good years to spend;
Longed to get home and join the careless crowd
Of chaps who work in peace with Time for friend.
That's all washed out now. You're beyond the wire:
No earthly chance can send you crawling back;
You've finished with machine-gun fire—
Knocked over in a hopeless dud-attack.

Somehow I always thought you'd get done in,
Because you were so desperate keen to live:
You were all out to try and save your skin,
Well knowing how much the world had got to give.
You joked at shells and talked the usual "shop,"
Stuck to your dirty job and did it fine:
With "Jesus Christ! when will it stop?
Three years.... It's hell unless we break their line."

So when they told me you'd been left for dead
I wouldn't believe them, feeling it must be true.
Next week the bloody Roll of Honour said
"Wounded and missing"—(That's the thing to do
When lads are left in shell-holes dying slow,
With nothing but blank sky and wounds that ache,
Moaning for water till they know
It's night, and then it's not worth while to wake!)

Good-bye, old lad! Remember me to God,
And tell Him that our Politicians swear
They won't give in till Prussian Rule's been trod
Under the Heel of England.... Are you there?...

Yes ... and the War won't end for at least two years;
But we've got stacks of men ... I'm blind with tears,
Staring into the dark. Cheero!
I wish they'd killed you in a decent show.

SICK LEAVE

When I'm asleep, dreaming and lulled and warm,—
They come, the homeless ones, the noiseless dead.
While the dim charging breakers of the storm
Bellow and drone and rumble overhead,
Out of the gloom they gather about my bed.
They whisper to my heart; their thoughts are mine.
"Why are you here with all your watches ended?
From Ypres to Frise we sought you in the Line."
In bitter safety I awake, unfriended;
And while the dawn begins with slashing rain
I think of the Battalion in the mud.
"When are you going out to them again?
Are they not still your brothers through our blood?"

BANISHMENT

I am banished from the patient men who fight.
They smote my heart to pity, built my pride.
Shoulder to aching shoulder, side by side,
They trudged away from life's broad wealds of light.
Their wrongs were mine; and ever in my sight
They went arrayed in honour. But they died,—
Not one by one: and mutinous I cried

To those who sent them out into the night.

The darkness tells how vainly I have striven
To free them from the pit where they must dwell
In outcast gloom convulsed and jagged and riven
By grappling guns. Love drove me to rebel.
Love drives me back to grope with them through hell;
And in their tortured eyes I stand forgiven.

AUTUMN

October's bellowing anger breaks and cleaves
The bronzed battalions of the stricken wood
In whose lament I hear a voice that grieves
For battle's fruitless harvest, and the feud
Of outraged men. Their lives are like the leaves
Scattered in flocks of ruin, tossed and blown
Along the westering furnace flaring red.
O martyred youth and manhood overthrown,
The burden of your wrongs is on my head.

REPRESSION OF WAR EXPERIENCE

Now light the candles; one; two; there's a moth;
What silly beggars they are to blunder in
And scorch their wings with glory, liquid flame—
No, no, not that,—it's bad to think of war,
When thoughts you've gagged all day come back to scare you;
And it's been proved that soldiers don't go mad
Unless they lose control of ugly thoughts
That drive them out to jabber among the trees.

Now light your pipe; look, what a steady hand.
Draw a deep breath; stop thinking; count fifteen,
And you're as right as rain.... Why won't it rain?...
I wish there'd be a thunder-storm to-night,
With bucketsful of water to sluice the dark,
And make the roses hang their dripping heads.

Books; what a jolly company they are,
Standing so quiet and patient on their shelves,
Dressed in dim brown, and black, and white, and green
And every kind of colour. Which will you read?
Come on; O do read something; they're so wise.

I tell you all the wisdom of the world
Is waiting for you on those shelves; and yet
You sit and gnaw your nails, and let your pipe out,
And listen to the silence: on the ceiling
There's one big, dizzy moth that bumps and flutters;
And in the breathless air outside the house
The garden waits for something that delays.
There must be crowds of ghosts among the trees,—
Not people killed in battle,—they're in France,—
But horrible shapes in shrouds—old men who died
Slow, natural deaths,—old men with ugly souls,
Who wore their bodies out with nasty sins.

You're quiet and peaceful, summering safe at home;
You'd never think there was a bloody war on!...
O yes, you would ... why, you can hear the guns.
Hark! Thud, thud, thud,—quite soft ... they never cease—
Those whispering guns—O Christ, I want to go out
And screech at them to stop—I'm going crazy;
I'm going stark, staring mad because of the guns.

TOGETHER

Splashing along the boggy woods all day,
And over brambled hedge and holding clay,
I shall not think of him:
But when the watery fields grow brown and dim,
And hounds have lost their fox, and horses tire,
I know that he'll be with me on my way
Home through the darkness to the evening fire.

He's jumped each stile along the glistening lanes;
His hand will be upon the mud-soaked reins;
Hearing the saddle creak,
He'll wonder if the frost will come next week.
I shall forget him in the morning light;
And while we gallop on he will not speak:
But at the stable-door he'll say good-night.

THE HAWTHORN TREE

Not much to me is yonder lane
Where I go every day;

But when there's been a shower of rain
And hedge-birds whistle gay,
I know my lad that's out in France
With fearsome things to see
Would give his eyes for just one glance
At our white hawthorn tree.

Not much to me is yonder lane
Where he so longs to tread;
But when there's been a shower of rain
I think I'll never weep again
Until I've heard he's dead.

CONCERT PARTY

(EGYPTIAN BASE CAMP)

They are gathering round ...
Out of the twilight; over the grey-blue sand,
Shoals of low-jargoning men drift inward to the sound,—
The jangle and throb of a piano ... tum-ti-tum ...
Drawn by a lamp, they come
Out of the glimmering lines of their tents, over the shuffling sand.

O sing us the songs, the songs of our own land,
You warbling ladies in white.
Dimness conceals the hunger in our faces,
This wall of faces risen out of the night,
These eyes that keep their memories of the places
So long beyond their sight.

Jaded and gay, the ladies sing; and the chap in brown
Tilts his grey hat; jaunty and lean and pale,
He rattles the keys ... some actor-bloke from town ...

"God send you home"; and then "A long, long trail";
"I hear you catting me"; and "Dixieland" ...
Sing slowly ... now the chorus ... one by one
We hear them, drink them; till the concert's done.
Silent, I watch the shadowy mass of soldiers stand.
Silent, they drift away, over the glimmering sand.

KANTARA,
April, 1918.

NIGHT ON THE CONVOY

(ALEXANDRIA-MARSEILLES)

Out in the blustering darkness, on the deck
A gleam of stars looks down. Long blurs of black,
The lean Destroyers, level with our track,
Plunging and stealing, watch the perilous way
Through backward racing seas and caverns of chill spray.

One sentry by the davits, in the gloom
Stands mute; the boat heaves onward through the night.
Shrouded is every chink of cabined light:
And sluiced by floundering waves that hiss and boom
And crash like guns, the troop-ship shudders ... doom.

Now something at my feet stirs with a sigh;
And slowly growing used to groping dark,
I know that the hurricane-deck, down all its length,
Is heaped and spread with lads in sprawling strength,—
Blanketed soldiers sleeping. In the stark
Danger of life at war, they lie so still,
All prostrate and defenceless, head by head ...
And I remember Arras, and that hill
Where dumb with pain I stumbled among the dead.

We are going home. The troop-ship, in a thrill
Of fiery-chamber'd anguish, throbs and rolls.
We are going home ... victims ... three thousand souls.

May, 1918.

A LETTER HOME

(To Robert Graves)

I

Here I'm sitting in the gloom
Of my quiet attic room.
France goes rolling all around,
Fledged with forest May has crowned.
And I puff my pipe, calm-hearted,
Thinking how the fighting started,
Wondering when we'll ever end it,

Back to Hell with Kaiser send it,
Gag the noise, pack up and go,
Clockwork soldiers in a row.
I've got better things to do
Than to waste my time on you.

II

Robert, when I drowse to-night,
Skirting lawns of sleep to chase
Shifting dreams in mazy light,
Somewhere then I'll see your face
Turning back to bid me follow
Where I wag my arms and hollo,
Over hedges hasting after
Crooked smile and baffling laughter,
Running tireless, floating, leaping,
Down your web-hung woods and valleys,
Garden glooms and hornbeam alleys,
Where the glowworm stars are peeping,
Till I find you, quiet as stone
On a hill-top all alone,
Staring outward, gravely pondering
Jumbled leagues of hillock-wandering.

III

You and I have walked together
In the starving winter weather.
We've been glad because we knew
Time's too short and friends are few.
We've been sad because we missed
One whose yellow head was kissed
By the gods, who thought about him
Till they couldn't do without him.
Now he's here again; I've seen
Soldier David dressed in green,
Standing in a wood that swings
To the madrigal he sings.
He's come back, all mirth and glory,
Like the prince in a fairy story.
Winter called him far away;
Blossoms bring him home with May.

IV

Well, I know you'll swear it's true
That you found him decked in blue
Striding up through morning-land
With a cloud on either hand.
Out in Wales, you'll say, he marches
Arm-in-arm with oaks and larches;
Hides all night in hilly nooks,
Laughs at dawn in tumbling brooks.
Yet, it's certain, here he teaches
Outpost-schemes to groups of beeches.
And I'm sure, as here I stand,
That he shines through every land,
That he sings in every place
Where we're thinking of his face.

V

Robert, there's a war in France;
Everywhere men bang and blunder,
Sweat and swear and worship Chance,
Creep and blink through cannon thunder.
Rifles crack and bullets flick,
Sing and hum like hornet-swarms.
Bones are smashed and buried quick.
Yet, through stunning battle storms.
All the while I watch the spark
Lit to guide me; for I know
Dreams will triumph, though the dark
Scowls above me where I go.
You can hear me; you can mingle
Radiant folly with my jingle,
War's a joke for me and you
While we know such dreams are true!

RECONCILIATION

When you are standing at your hero's grave,
Or near some homeless village where he died,
Remember, through your heart's rekindling pride,
The German soldiers who were loyal and brave.

Men fought like brutes; and hideous things were done:
And you have nourished hatred, harsh and blind.
But in that Golgotha perhaps you'll find

The mothers of the men who killed your son.

November, 1918.

MEMORIAL TABLET

(GREAT WAR)

Squire nagged and bullied till I went to fight
(Under Lord Derby's scheme). I died in hell—
(They called it Passchendaele); my wound was slight,
And I was hobbling back, and then a shell
Burst slick upon the duck-boards; so I fell
Into the bottomless mud, and lost the light.

In sermon-time, while Squire is in his pew,
He gives my gilded name a thoughtful stare;
For though low down upon the list, I'm there:
"In proud and glorious memory"—that's my due.
Two bleeding years I fought in France for Squire;
I suffered anguish that he's never guessed;
Once I came home on leave; and then went west.
What greater glory could a man desire?

THE DEATH-BED

He drowsed and was aware of silence heaped
Round him, unshaken as the steadfast walls;
Aqueous like floating rays of amber light,
Soaring and quivering in the wings of sleep,—
Silence and safety; and his mortal shore
Lipped by the inward, moonless waves of death.

Some one was holding water to his mouth.
He swallowed, unresisting; moaned and dropped
Through crimson gloom to darkness; and forgot
The opiate throb and ache that was his wound.
Water—calm, sliding green above the weir;
Water—a sky-lit alley for his boat,
Bird-voiced, and bordered with reflected flowers
And shaken hues of summer: drifting down,
He dipped contented oars, and sighed, and slept.

Night, with a gust of wind, was in the ward,

Blowing the curtain to a glimmering curve.
Night. He was blind; he could not see the stars
Glinting among the wraiths of wandering cloud;
Queer blots of colour, purple, scarlet, green,
Flickered and faded in his drowning eyes.

Rain; he could hear it rustling through the dark;
Fragrance and passionless music woven as one;
Warm rain on drooping roses; pattering showers
That soak the woods; not the harsh rain that sweeps
Behind the thunder, but a trickling peace
Gently and slowly washing life away.

He stirred, shifting his body; then the pain
Leaped like a prowling beast, and gripped and tore
His groping dreams with grinding claws and fangs.
But some one was beside him; soon he lay
Shuddering because that evil thing had passed.
And Death, who'd stepped toward him, paused and stared.

Light many lamps and gather round his bed.
Lend him your eyes, warm blood, and will to live.
Speak to him; rouse him; you may save him yet.
He's young; he hated war; how should he die
When cruel old campaigners win safe through?

But Death replied: "I choose him." So he went,
And there was silence in the summer night;
Silence and safety; and the veils of sleep.
Then, far away, the thudding of the guns.

AFTERMATH

Have you forgotten yet?...
For the world's events have rumbled on since those gagged days,
Like traffic checked awhile at the crossing of city ways:
And the haunted gap in your mind has filled with thoughts that flow
Like clouds in the lit heavens of life; and you're a man reprieved to go,
Taking your peaceful share of Time, with joy to spare.
But the past is just the same,—and War's a bloody game,...
Have you forgotten yet?...
Look down, and swear by the slain of the War that you'll never forget.

Do you remember the dark months you held the sector at Mametz,—
The nights you watched and wired and dug and piled sandbags on parapets?
Do you remember the rats; and the stench

Of corpses rotting in front of the front-line trench,—
And dawn coming, dirty-white, and chill with a hopeless rain?
Do you ever stop and ask, "Is it all going to happen again?"

Do you remember that hour of din before the attack,—
And the anger, the blind compassion that seized and shook you then
As you peered at the doomed and haggard faces of your men?
Do you remember the stretcher-cases lurching back
With dying eyes and lolling heads,—those ashen-grey
Masks of the lads who once were keen and kind and gay?

Have you forgotten yet?...
Look up, and swear by the green of the Spring that you'll never forget.

SONG-BOOKS OF THE WAR

In fifty years, when peace outshines
Remembrance of the battle lines,
Adventurous lads will sigh and cast
Proud looks upon the plundered past.
On summer morn or winter's night,
Their hearts will kindle for the fight,
Reading a snatch of soldier-song,
Savage and jaunty, fierce and strong;
And through the angry marching rhymes
Of blind regret and haggard mirth,
They'll envy us the dazzling times
When sacrifice absolved our earth.

Some ancient man with silver locks
Will lift his weary face to say:
"War was a fiend who stopped our clocks
Although we met him grim and gay."
And then he'll speak of Haig's last drive,
Marvelling that any came alive
Out of the shambles that men built
And smashed, to cleanse the world of guilt.
But the boys, with grin and sidelong glance,
Will think, "Poor grandad's day is done."
And dream of lads who fought in France
And lived in time to share the fun.

EVERYONE SANG

Everyone suddenly burst out singing;
And I was filled with such delight
As prisoned birds must find in freedom
Winging wildly across the white
Orchards and dark green fields; on; on; and out of sight.

Everyone's voice was suddenly lifted,
And beauty came like the setting sun.
My heart was shaken with tears and horror
Drifted away ... O but every one
Was a bird; and the song was wordless; the singing will never be done.

April, 1919.

Siegfried Sassoon – A Short Biography

Siegfried Loraine Sassoon was born on 8th September 1886. He grew up in the neo-gothic mansion 'Weirleigh', in Matfield, Kent.

His father, Alfred Ezra Sassoon, was a member of the wealthy Baghdadi Jewish Sassoon merchant family. For marrying outside the faith he was disinherited. His mother, Theresa, was from the Anglo-Catholic Thornycroft family, the sculptors responsible for many of the best-known statues in London. Interestingly she named him Siegfried because of her love for Wagner's operas rather than any German ancestry. He was the second of three sons. When he was four years old his parents separated.

Sassoon was educated at the New Beacon School, Sevenoaks, Kent then Marlborough College, Wiltshire and finally at Clare College, Cambridge, where from 1905 to 1907 he read history. He went down from Cambridge without a degree and spent the next few years indulging himself hunting, playing cricket and writing verse: some of which he published privately. Sassoon had only a small private income that, provided he lived modestly, negated the need to work, though in later years he would be left a generous legacy by his aunt, Rachel Beer, allowing him to buy the estate of Heytesbury House in Wiltshire.

His first published success, 'The Daffodil Murderer' (1913), was a parody of John Masefield's 'The Everlasting Mercy'. His great friend Robert Graves describes it as a "parody of Masefield which, midway through, had forgotten to be a parody and turned into rather good Masefield."

Sassoon was a good amateur cricketer and was keen to play for Kent County Cricket Club. He often turned out for the Bluemantles, where he sometimes played alongside another keen cricketer, Arthur Conan Doyle. Although an enthusiast, Sassoon was not good enough to play for Kent, but he continued to play cricket into his seventies.

Sassoon had proffered his opinions on the political situation before the First World War thus—"France was a lady, Russia was a bear, and performing in the county cricket team was much more important than either of them".

However, motivated by patriotism, Sassoon joined the British Army as the threat of war escalated. He was in service with the Sussex Yeomanry on 4th August 1914, the day war was declared on Germany.

He broke his arm badly in a riding accident and was therefore out of action before even leaving England. He spent the spring of 1915 convalescing. Sassoon was commissioned into the 3rd Battalion (Special Reserve), Royal Welch Fusiliers, as a second lieutenant on 29th May 1915. On 1st November his younger brother Hamo was killed in the Gallipoli Campaign, and that same month Sassoon was sent to the 1st Battalion in France. There he met Robert Graves, and they became close friends, drawn together by their poetic ambitions, they would read and discuss each other's work. Graves' views on what may be called 'gritty realism' profoundly affected Sassoon's idea of what poetry was. Life on the front line meant he soon became horrified by the slaughter and daily realities of war, and the tone of his writing changed dramatically: where his early poems exhibit a Romantic, dilettantish sweetness, his war poetry moves to an increasingly discordant beat, stridently conveying the ugly truths of the trenches to an audience hitherto placated by jingoistic and patriotic propaganda.

Conversely Sassoon's periods of duty on the Western Front were marked by exceptionally brave actions, including the single-handed capture of a German trench in the Hindenburg Line. Armed with grenades, he scattered sixty German soldiers.

Sassoon's bravery was so inspiring that his fellow soldiers said they felt confident only when they were accompanied by him. He often went out on night-raids and bombing patrols and demonstrated ruthless efficiency as a company commander. Deepening depression at the horror and misery the soldiers were forced to endure produced in Sassoon a paradoxically manic courage, and earned him the nickname 'Mad Jack' by his men for his many and near-suicidal exploits. On 27th July 1916 Sassoon was awarded the Military Cross. He was also later recommended for the Victoria Cross.

His poetry both described the horrors of the trenches and satirised the patriotic pretensions of those who, in Sassoon's view, were responsible for a jingoism-fuelled war.

Despite his decorations and reputation, in 1917 Sassoon decided to make a stand against the running of the war. At the end of a spell of convalescent leave, Sassoon declined to return to duty; instead, encouraged by pacifist friends such as Bertrand Russell and Lady Ottoline Morrell, he sent a letter to his commanding officer entitled 'Finished with the War: A Soldier's Declaration'. Forwarded to the press and read out in the House of Commons by a sympathetic member of Parliament, the letter was seen by some as treasonous ('I am making this statement as an act of wilful defiance of military authority') and by others as condemning the war government's motives ('I believe that the war upon which I entered as a war of defence and liberation has now become a war of aggression and conquest'). Rather than court-martial Sassoon, the authorities decided that he was unfit for service and had him sent to Craiglockhart War Hospital near Edinburgh. This facility had opened in 1916 as a military psychiatric hospital to care for officers suffering from the psychological effects of the Great War, such as neurasthenia ('shell shock').

At Craiglockhart, Sassoon met Wilfred Owen, a poet who would eventually exceed him in fame. It was perhaps thanks to Sassoon that Owen persevered in his ambition to write better poetry. Both men returned to active service in France. Owen would later be killed in 1918, just a week before Armistice. Sassoon, despite all this, was promoted to lieutenant, and having spent some time away from danger in Palestine, eventually returned to the front line.

On 13th July 1918, Sassoon was almost immediately wounded again—by friendly fire when he was shot in the head by a British soldier who had mistaken him for a German near Arras, France. As a result, he spent the remaining months of the war in Britain. By this time he had been promoted to acting captain.

On 12th March 1919 Sassoon relinquished his commission on health grounds but was allowed to retain the rank of captain.

He now dabbled briefly in the politics of the Labour movement which was now gathering strength after the first two tumultuous decades of the 20th Century.

In 1919 took up a post as literary editor of the socialist Daily Herald. Here he was responsible for employing several eminent names as reviewers, including E. M. Forster and Charlotte Mew. Sassoon also commissioned new material from the likes of Arnold Bennett and Osbert Sitwell. He also managed to now extend his own interests to include music.

Sassoon now accepted a lecture tour of the United States and travelled throughout Europe and across Britain. He came into possession of a car, a gift from the publisher Frankie Schuster. He became renowned among his friends for his poor driving skills, which apparently did not discourage him from making full use of the car.

In 1923 he visited Wales. Sassoon was a great admirer of the Welsh poet Henry Vaughan and paid a pilgrimage to his grave at Llansantffraed, Powys. It was there he wrote one of his best-known peacetime poems, 'At the Grave of Henry Vaughan'.

Unhappily there came the deaths in quick succession of three of his closest friends; Edmund Gosse, Thomas Hardy and Frankie Schuster, causing a serious setback to his personal happiness.

Sassoon was now, in 1928, preparing to take a new direction by branching out into prose, with 'Memoirs of a Fox-Hunting Man'. This anonymously published first volume of a fictionalised autobiography, was acclaimed as a classic, bringing its author fame as a humorous writer. The book won the 1928 James Tait Black Award for fiction. Sassoon followed it with 'Memoirs of an Infantry Officer' (1930) and 'Sherston's Progress' (1936). Some time later he would write his own autobiography based on his youth and early manhood across three volumes, which were also widely acclaimed. These were 'The Old Century', 'The Weald of Youth' and 'Siegfried's Journey'.

Sassoon, having matured greatly as a result of his military service, continued to seek long-lasting, loving relationships. Initially these were with a succession of men.

In September 1931, Sassoon rented Fitz House, Teffont Magna, Wiltshire and began to live there. In December 1933, he married Hester Gatty, who was many years his junior. The marriage led to the birth of a child, George, which he had craved for a long time.

By 1945 Sassoon was separated from his wife and was living in seclusion at Heytesbury in Wiltshire, although he continued to keep contact with a circle which included E.M. Forster and J.R. Ackerley. One of his closest friends was the cricketer, Dennis Silk who would become Warden (headmaster) of Radley College. He also formed a close friendship with Vivien Hancock, the headmistress of Greenways School at Ashton Gifford, where his son George was a pupil. This provoked Hester to make strong accusations against her who then responded with a threat of legal action.

In his last years Sassoon converted to Roman Catholicism. He had hoped that Ronald Knox, a Roman Catholic priest and writer whom he admired, would instruct him in the faith, but Knox was too ill to take on the task. The priest Sebastian Moore was chosen to instruct him instead, and Sassoon was admitted to the faith at Downside Abbey in Somerset. He also paid regular visits to the nuns at Stanbrook Abbey, and their press printed commemorative editions of some of his poems.

Sassoon was appointed Commander of the Order of the British Empire (CBE) in the 1951 New Year Honours.

Siegfried Loraine Sassoon, CBE, MC died from stomach cancer on 1st September 1967, a week before his 81st birthday. He is buried at St Andrew's Church, Mells, Somerset.

On 11th November 1985, Sassoon was among sixteen Great War poets commemorated on a slate stone unveiled in Westminster Abbey's Poet's Corner. The inscription on the stone was written by friend and fellow War poet Wilfred Owen. It reads: "My subject is War, and the pity of War. The Poetry is in the pity."

Siegried Sassoon – A Concise Bibliography

Poetry
The Daffodil Murderer (1913)
The Old Huntsman and Other Poems (1917)
Counter-Attack and Other Poems (1918)
The War Poems of Siegfried Sassoon (1919)
Picture-Show (1919)
Recreations (1923)
Lingual Exercises for Advanced Vocabularians (1925)
Selected Poems (1925)
Satirical Poems (1926)
The Heart's Journey (1928)
Poems by Pinchbeck Lyre (1931)
The Road to Ruin (1933)
Vigils (1935)
Rhymed Ruminations (1940)
Poems Newly Selected (1940)
Collected Poems (1947)
Common Chords (1950/1951)
Emblems of Experience (1951)
The Tasking (1954)
Sequences (1956)
Lenten Illuminations (1959)
The Path to Peace (1960)
Collected Poems 1908-1956 (1961)
The War Poems ed. Rupert Hart-Davis (1983)

Prose

Memoirs of a Fox-Hunting Man (1928)
Memoirs of an Infantry Officer (1930)
Sherston's Progress (1936)
Complete Memoirs of George Sherston (1937)
The Old Century (1938)
On Poetry (1939)
The Weald of Youth (1942)
Siegfried's Journey (1945)
Meredith (1948)

Other Works

Finished with the War: A Soldier's Declaration (1917)
"Introduction" to Poems by Wilfred Owen (1920)

Made in the USA
Middletown, DE
31 January 2020